# TRANSFERRING ENTHUSIASM

## The Sales Book For Your Business Growth

### JULIE FAIRHURST

# TRANSFERRING ENTHUSIASM

---

## THE SALES BOOK FOR YOUR BUSINESS GROWTH

## JULIE FAIRHURST

ROCK STAR PUBLISHING

# CONTENTS

...

"I never dreamed about success. I worked for it."

Estée Lauder

# INTRODUCTION

## IS YOUR LACK OF SALES GIVING YOU SLEEPLESS NIGHTS?

I can totally relate! When I first started in sales, I struggled daily and thought of quitting often. I wondered if I should get a "real job." I decided to stick with it and became 100% committed to my success.

Do not underestimate yourself! If I can do it, so can you. I know you have heard that before, but it is the truth. Things can turn around, and I am the proof.

I went from standing in line at food banks and living off government handouts to becoming a multi-award-winning top sales professional. I built the life I dreamed of with over 2,500 thousand clients and sold over $250,000 million in sales.

How can this book benefit you? By shifting your mindset, learning to sell without selling, nurturing clients who say no, and discovering what taking action can do for you.

This is an opportunity to shift your success! I am super excited for you to get started. Be sure to have a journal handy to answer your discovery questions and make important notes you can refer back to.

My wish for you is that you stop struggling and begin to live your best life—the life you have always desired for yourself.

Julie Fairhurst

"Business opportunities are like buses,
there's always another one coming."
Richard Branson

# PART 1

# 1

## POVERTY OR PROSPERITY?

### WHAT MINDSET DO YOU HAVE?

"The pessimist sees difficulty in every opportunity.
The optimist sees opportunity in every difficulty."
Winston Churchill

### *Where do your beliefs come from?*

Have you ever given this some thought? Where did you get the beliefs that you have?

If you are like most of us, you will accept the beliefs passed down by your past generations. You adopted the ideas of your parents. Your parents took their parent's opinions, and so on, usually without ever questioning or realizing that they were even doing it.

What beliefs did your family pass on to you regarding money and success? When I grew up most of the time, well almost always, with our families surviving on the government welfare system, some strong messages came with growing up in that environment.

***The messages I heard were...***

- Those damn rich people don't care about anyone but themselves.
- I'm not made of money.
- Money doesn't grow on trees.
- If it weren't for you kids, I wouldn't always be so broke.
- We can't afford it.
- We can't buy anything until our welfare check comes in,

It was never the fault of anyone in my family for the way we lived. I never heard anyone say I had better go out there and get a job so that I can support my family. I grew up in a home of scarcity and lack.

And when you live in that environment, year after year, you will naturally have the beliefs of those who took care of you. As a child, those beliefs will become your beliefs.

***What can negative beliefs do to your mindset?***

- You feel unworthy.
- You think you don't deserve good things.
- You think you can't achieve success.
- You think you don't deserve money.

- You were in a constant state of anxiety and depression.
- You may wonder why bad things happen to you.
- You may blame others for your situation.
- You live in the past, unable to move forward.
- You see yourself as a victim.

These were some of the ways I felt and thought while growing up. When I did try to do anything outside my comfort zone, I felt like a fraud and was in a state of anxiety that someone would be able to see the inside of me and call me out on being such a fraud.

### *Discovery Journal*

- What are some of the beliefs that your family has handed you down?
- Right out your beliefs of them as you can think of.
- How many of those beliefs are different from your family's?

### *How do you change your core beliefs that are not serving you?*

Your core beliefs are how you see yourself and, how you judge yourself, how you see the world. You were living your life with negative thoughts about yourself, money success, and your beliefs are possibly working against you.

### *Beliefs are just the thoughts you think!*

The good news is that you can change your beliefs by being conscientious of your thoughts. Pay attention during the day. How do you feel about yourself? How do you perceive successful people?

I am sharing some of the past messages which will work for you because they have helped me develop positive beliefs. The good news is that new thoughts create new beliefs.

- I am responsible for me.
- I can do whatever I desire.
- I see possibilities everywhere I go.
- People are always ready to be helpful to me.
- I am worthy and deserving.
- People want to do business with me.
- Money flows easily and freely to me.
- I always have more than enough than I need.

### *Taking action!*

Changing your beliefs and thoughts is imperative for moving toward the success you desire. However, it doesn't stop there. You can't just change your beliefs and then lay around the house watching TV all day. Taking action is the next step in moving toward the life you want.

I remember conversing with a girlfriend when she was complaining about not dating anyone for quite some time. She needed to put herself out there more to meet new people. I told her, you can't sit around your apartment and wait for him to knock on the door. Get up and get out there.

It worked. She decided to take action and met her future husband at a local coffee shop.

Start taking action today. The universe has your back but cannot do the work for you. Only you can take action.

### *Discovery Journal*

- Write ten positive messages for yourself that will help you change your beliefs.

Once you have written them out, you can then put them on sticky notes and put them in different areas of your home or workplace so you can view them several times a day.

Keep the list by your bed, and instead of reaching for your phone first thing in the morning when you wake up, reach for your list. Please read it before you do anything else.

You will be amazed at how it will work in helping you shift your mindset from a negative to a positive one.

This is an excellent quote by Napoleon Hill. I read it daily!

"Whatever the mind can conceive and believe, it can achieve."

...

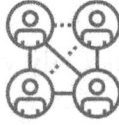

"Every problem is a gift—without problems,
we would not grow."

Anthony Robbins

# 2

# CAN YOU SELL WITHOUT SELLING?

"The elevator to success is out of order.
You'll have to use the stairs, one step at a time."
Joe Girard

***How do you feel when you think of having to sell something?***

The thought of being a salesperson, or the view of selling something to someone, can bring up an unpleasant feeling for some. They hate the idea of selling or being thought of as a salesperson.

I was there! At the beginning of my sales career, I did everything I could to avoid the word sales representative on my business card. I was embarrassed to tell anyone I was in sales, and until I turned my mindset around, I will tell you selling was a tough job.

Let us change your perspective on selling if that is where you are. It is not scary or icky.

We have all had bad experiences with salespeople. You know, the ones who are pushy, not listening to the buyer's concerns and making it all about them. The good news is that those salespeople are far between these days. The sales process has evolved and grown in an effective way.

***What is your definition of sales?***

"Sales is the transfer of enthusiasm."

Are you enthusiastic about what you are selling? If so, is your enthusiasm contagious?

The buyer feels it and gets excited about the opportunity to make the purchase and buy the product. Tell them enthusiastically if you think this will fit their needs and be a good fit! BUT... do not try to be excited if you're not. The buyer or your prospective client will be turned off by anything that appears phony. Be authentic and genuine in your enthusiasm. Just be you, and you will do just fine.

***Marketing is sales.***

This is a gentle way of selling your product or service. You market it. You advertise it. You get in front of your potential buyer or client and let the product or the marketing speak for you.

Buyers are well informed more than at any other time. They will make their own decision when it comes to making the purchase. They will not be pushed into making a rash decision. And that's good news for you because you do not need to worry about selling them into something. You will present the service or product, and they will make their decision.

*Ask yourself if you know the answers to these questions. You should.*

- What are their needs?
- What is it that your buyer needs?
- Why do they need to buy the product or service?

If you can answer those questions, then you are off and running.

Figure out what people need, then offer it to them. If there is a need for your product or service when you put it out there, they will come and inquire and then buy.

Understanding your buyer's needs will help you move toward how to market your product or service to your buyer. If they do not need it or don't need your service, then, of course, they're not buying, period. Get into the core of their needs and present how you or how your product can help, and the sale will flow smoothly.

## *Discovery Journal*

- Make some notes about what your buyer or prospective client's needs are.
- Write out as many as you can think of. It will help when you are developing your marketing plan.

### *See yourself as their guide.*

The prospective buyer or client needs you to guide them through the process of buying from you. You will be guiding them to the service or product, guiding them through the understanding of why they need what you are offering. Then you guide them to make the purchase or enter into a service contract with you.

Have you ever been surprised at what you do not know? I am always shocked that I had no idea about what I have just learned when I learn something completely new. I am amazed to think of all the things I don't know.

Well, your prospective buyer or client is in the same situation. They do not know what they don't know. This is why they need you to be their guide so that they can learn.

Maybe they don't even know they have a need. You have a chance to guide them to an awakening of what their needs are and how you can help them achieve those needs. Help them solve the problem they may not even know they have.

### *Make it all about them!*

Have you ever had to sit through a conversation with the salesperson (or anyone for that matter) who makes it all about them? It is like you are their captive audience; all you can do is think of how you can escape the situation.

Be customer focused. Focus on them: their needs and their wants.

Listen. Listening is so essential. Many people feel they need to be heard; make sure you hear your potential buyer or client. Let them feel and know that you have listened to them, you get what they are saying, and you care.

Ask appropriate questions about what they need, what they want, and how they see things. By asking questions and letting them answer, you are proving to them that you care and want to make this about them and their needs.

Be honest with them. Tell them if you feel it is not a good fit for them. The trust you will build will be immense. Do not let them purchase if you don't believe it's genuinely going to help them.

Being honest and making it about them, not about you, will create a fan for life. This will give you an opportunity to ask for a referral or to pass your name to someone they feel would be a good fit working with you or buying your product.

Use this rule whenever you are engaging with a prospective buyer or client. This is my 80/20 Rule for sales.

Make it 80% about them and 20% about you or the product.

Do not be afraid to talk about yourself. They want to get to know you and understand you and the product. Just remember this 80/20 rule, follow it, and you will do great. They will love you!

### How will you keep in contact with your new fan?

When you have something you feel is a good fit for them, you will let them know about the opportunity. And because you have been honest with them, they will trust you, believe you, and be willing to do business with you.

Once you have mastered the art of making it about your perspective client or buyer, be sure to slide in here and there what you were offering to do for them. Even though it is all about them, you can still engage them with the offer. Your product or service is the reason you are in contact with them, so of course, they are expecting you to have a discussion with them about it.

### Offer them solutions or options.

If you have now realized that what you have been offering is not suitable for your buyer or prospective client, then who does have what they need? Be helpful to them. If you know what would work for them, tell them, and connect them to the other product or service they need.

This is your opportunity to shine! Network with others, be aware of what they have to offer, and when you come across that potential client, if you think they would be a good fit, this is the time to make a referral.

Work on a referral plan with others. Let us help one another along the way. There is nothing wrong with being paid a referral fee for referring a business to others.

***Build your network.***

Building a network of like-minded people who offer various programs and solutions. Discuss referral fees with them. What can you do to help each other? The big companies are doing this. They see the value in having others refer their products or services. And they are willing to pay for those referrals.

Why don't we do it as well? It helps the prospective buyer or our client. It gives the other person business. At the same time, it helps us by putting a little money back in our pockets as well. It can be a win-win for everyone!

## *Discovery Journal*

- Write down whom you could network with for referrals.
- Whom would you trust with your referrals?
- Find people or products that you can positively support and believe in.

Another great quote that has helped in when I have struggled. This one is by the outstanding Zig Ziglar.

"Your attitude, not your aptitude, will determine your altitude."

...

"You only have to do a few things right in your life so long as you don't do too many things wrong."

Warren Buffett

# 3

---

# ASKING FOR THE BUSINESS

"Opportunities don't happen, you create them."
Chris Grosser

Are you asking for the business? Asking for the business can be uncomfortable.

The problem is that you may only get it if you ask. When you ask for the business, you may be pleasantly surprised at how many yeses you will get. When you ask, the universe does respond.

You are not alone if you are not asking for the business or the sale!

"40% of salespeople say asking for the business is the most challenging part of the sales process" (HubSpot)

"64% of salespeople don't close. Sales management is shocked into disbelief by the 64% statistic; others say the number probably is too low!"
(Action Selling)

Let us look at why we don't ask. You have spent so much energy, money, and effort to get in front of your prospective buyer or client. Why would you not ask?

- Fear of rejection. This is huge. What if you were told no? You will have to wrap your head around this one. Just because you hear no does not mean they're rejecting you. No can mean many things; in the end, it might have nothing to do with you.
- Fear they will say yes. If they say yes, now what? Here you may be anxious about whether you can deliver your promise to them. If they say yes now, I will have to deliver. This can also be a fear of success and sabotaging yourself.
- You do not know how to ask. You may be asking the wrong questions. Not knowing how to ask can stop you from asking.
- You are uncomfortable. Possibly you are unsure about sales? You may have experienced negative thoughts about what sales are and what you think of salespeople. Maybe you had a bad experience with a salesperson or the sales process, and now you need to learn how to approach your prospect.

- You may want to avoid putting the other person on the spot by asking them for business.

### *Discovery Journal*

- Now is a great time to journal about your feelings, your fear, or your resistance to asking for a commitment from your perspective buyer or client.
- What comes up for you when you think about asking for the business or sale?
- Explore any situations when you felt you should have asked but didn't.

### *Your prospective buyer or client wants you to ask... no, really, they do!*

Would you be surprised to know that your perspective client or buyer wants you to ask them? Yes, they really do. Why? Because they may be uncomfortable themselves and not sure how to move forward with the program or purchase, they may be unsure of how to start the conversation with you.

So often, we think it is about us; however, it is usually about them. They need you to ask them. If you do not, then you are not giving them the opportunity to say "YES."

In sales, it is all about your prospective client or buyer and always and never about you. You need to know that by asking if they want to buy, proceed, continue, or move forward. You are doing them a service and making it easier on them. Sure, you will get some who say, "no, thank you." And when you do, that is okay because you gave them the opportunity, and they were able to make their own intelligent decision as to what was right for them at that time.

If you do not ask, you really are not doing them or yourself any favors. Allow your prospective client or buyer to ask questions, make up their own minds, and give you their answer. This will only happen when you give them a chance by opening the dialogue with them.

And remember, once you have asked, you close your lips and be quiet and look to your prospect for an answer. This could take a few moments. It could even take a minute, but you must give them the opportunity to speak first. So often we lose the sale because we speak too quickly.

Silence for many of us can be uncomfortable, so we do not let the silence last long before we interject back into the conversation again. We do ourselves and our clients our prospective clients a disservice by not giving them an opportunity to give us their answers.

***Example:***

I went for an appointment at a salon to have a hair treatment. I loved the hairdresser, she did an excellent job, and I was planning on coming back again. As I was paying and getting ready to leave the salon, the hairdresser turned to me and said, "Would you like to book your next appointment." As I stood there, I thought I wanted to, but I wondered about my schedule. I was about to say, "Yes, let's book it," when she said, "Oh, don't worry about it. You can just give us a phone call when you are ready."

That woman lost me as a client because she did not let me think about what I was going to do. She spoke too soon and let me off the hook. And for whatever reason, I never went back.

Always let your client prospective client speak first after you have asked them if they want to do business with you or if they want to make the purchase. Remember! If you do not ask the answer is already no, which means you have lost before you started.

### *How can you ask for the commitment?*

Just ask. Isn't it simple? Just ask the question.

Be sure it is the right time to be asking. As you get comfortable asking, you will be able to feel if it is a suitable time. Your intuition will kick in. Listen to it.

I like to use, "would you like to proceed with the paperwork"? When the conversation or presentation is over, it is an obvious question. And remember, after you ask, do not say a word. Let them think about it and give you their answer. No matter how uncomfortable the silence is, wait for the answer.

Practice makes perfect—practice asking. The more you ask, the easier it will be when the time comes. When you ask with confidence in your voice, your prospect will take notice, and more often than not, you will hear that yes.

### Are you asking yes or no questions?

Not asking questions that open more dialogue with the potential buyer or client. At this stage, if they have all the information, you are looking for a one-word answer, preferably a yes.

Be clear and direct as to what you are asking them. Do not leave room for confusion. Remember you were looking for a one-word answer, so be sure to be clear.

"Are you ready to proceed with the paperwork?" "Are you ready to make the purchase?"

You are looking for a yes or no!

### Ask multiple times.

I have a program where I send a letter to a prospective client four times. Letter one goes out the first week. Letter two goes out the second week. Letter three goes out in the third week. Letter four goes out in the fourth week.

Usually, I will hear from the prospect by the third letter. After the fourth time, if the prospect does not enter into doing business with me, I put them on my contact list and connect with them in three months. If still not ready, every six months thereafter. Fifty percent of my business has come from this strategy. It works, but you have to be consistent.

You may have a prospect that says, "connect with me in six months or a year from now, and I'll see where I'm at." If this happens to you, make sure you connect with them four months in rather than six or eight months rather than twelve. It has been my experience that prospective buyers and clients tend to be ready a little sooner than they anticipated. If you are not asking for the business, the person who is in front of them will be the one that does.

Now do not hound them or become a pest because that will just make them mad and possibly tell you to stop contacting them, and you'll lose them as a potential customer. Be gentle, be consistent, be kind and consider it in your follow-up communications with them.

***What are other salespeople doing out there?***

- 60% of customers say no four times before saying yes.
- 48% of salespeople only make a single follow-up attempt.
- 44% of salespeople give up after one follow-up call.

(These statistics are from www.invespcro.com)

Hey, do not look at these statistics and feel down like it is so hard! This is a positive because, in sales, you can quickly rise to the top above your competitors if you ask for the business and follow up.

***How many times do I need to ask?***

This will depend on whom you are asking. You will feel and know if just one time is enough for this prospective client or buyer or if you should be asking for a further time. There is a lot of information out there about how often you need to ask. The most common advice would be three to four or even five times before someone will give you a yes.

You may feel better knowing you are not the only one who has to ask multiple times for what you want.

- Legend says that Colonel Sanders from Kentucky fried chicken had to go through 1,009 no's before he finally got a yes to his secret recipe.
- Twenty-seven publishers rejected Doctor Seuss's Mulberry Street before being accepted by Vanguard Press.
- It took J.K. Rolling two years to get the Harry Potter book published. Twelve different publishers rejected it before ending up with Bloomsbury.

Stay in integrity! Never do anything out of character. This does not mean I hate asking, so I will never ask. It means to ask with integrity and in alignment with your principles and values.

At the beginning of my sales career, I was told by my sales manager that I needed to be more aggressive in asking for the business. I thought, okay, I will try it and do what I am told. I was timid and nervous about asking for the business.

Well, that was a huge mistake! Big gigantic mistake! I ticked off the prospective client because I was being pushy and felt horrible because I was not working with my own integrity. Being pushy was not in my nature, and I made a complete mess of the situation. The prospective client got so angry that he slammed his fist on the table, leaned off his chair looked me straight in the eye to tell me he was not going to be doing business with me.

Be sure you are working with your integrity. It is so important. There are people out there for everyone. With over seven billion people on the planet, there is not a lack of perspective buyers or clients out there. If the one situation you are in does not feel right, then it's not right. You need to do what you think is right for you, work within your integrity then ask for the business.

### What do you do when you get that? Yes!

What you do next is get the signature and get the commitment in writing. Move forward with their yes to enter into the agreement with you. Now was not the time to continue talking about your services or talking about the product. Now is the time to get the paperwork signed and pat yourself on the back that you did a great job. And leave the meeting!

Always use the word agreement rather than contract. What is the difference? Nothing, they mean the same thing, but the word agreement sounds less scary.

### Don't ever burn a bridge!

So, you have asked, and it's 100% and "no." They are not moving forward with you. Now what? Just leave it alone and respect their no.

Do not take it personally, even if they enter into business with someone else. They may come back to you at a later time when they are ready. I have had clients start out many times with others. Only to be dissatisfied and come back to me. Always be kind and gentle with them. You may never know what will happen in the future.

There have been several times in my career when I did not get the business, and the client went to work with someone else. I always wish them well and never say anything negative about the fact that they decided to work with someone else. I cannot even tell you how many of those people came back to me when it didn't work out with the other person they chose to work with. Had I made them feel bad or made a big deal about not choosing to work with me, they would have ended up going to someone else.

Remember, people want to work with people who make them feel good, so be very careful about the words you choose or the energy you put out if you've been told no. Do not ever burn a bridge.

### *Discovery Journal*

- Write down some thoughts you have about how you could ask for the business.
- What do you feel comfortable doing?

- What do you feel uncomfortable doing?
- What are you going to do if you're told no?

Steve Harvey's quote about asking and believing is one you should start to use in your life.

"Ask! Believe! Receive! Focus on those three things."

...

"There's no shortage of remarkable ideas, what's missing is the will to execute them."

Seth Godin

# 4

---

# IT'S A BUSINESS DECISION

"One of the differences between some successful and
unsuccessful people is that one group is full of doers, while
the other is full of wishers."
Edmond Mabika

Is your prospect looking for a deal? If they are asking you
for a discount, do you understand why they're asking you?
Their why can make a difference as to whether you give
them that discount or not? It's so important to understand the
mindset of your prospective buyer or client so you know
how to respond appropriately without losing the sale.

Here are a few reasons they may be asking for that discount
from you.

- Possibly, they don't believe in your value.
- They do not have enough money.

- They may not understand what they are buying.
- They may not respect your time.
- Possibly, they just may like to haggle.
- They never pay full price for anything.
- They have succeeded in getting lower prices in the past.

Discounting is a business decision that only you can make. If you are just starting out and you need to be able to say you have actually worked with others or sold a product, then you will need to decide what you want to do. You were going to have to decide if you were going to give a discount to kick-start your business.

If money is tight, you may want to give a discount to start to bring in some business and release some of the financial stress that you are carrying around right now. Giving a discount could go one of two ways. It could end up being a really great business decision, or it can be a big mistake.

Sometimes you may want to keep it to yourself if you gave a discount rather than sharing it in a group or with others. Only some may be supportive of your decision.

I gave a discount once to a seller. A friend of mine gave me a tough time about giving the discount. I felt stupid and not very good about myself at the time for giving it. But hey! My friend was doing simply fine in her world and was not struggling, plus she had the help of a spouse who had a full-time job.

Here I was, trying to make it in the world of sales, where it can be super competitive, alone raising my three boys with an empty bank account. I needed to survive, and if that meant giving a discount to kick-start my business, then that is just what I was going to do.

After that negative reaction, if I ever gave a discount, I did keep it to myself as much as I could. I decided that I did not need any negativity surrounding my business decisions.

Have the conversation. Be sure to have an honest and open conversation with your potential client before making your decision. The last thing you want is to discount your price and then have this client not respect your time, your money, your worth, or your abilities. However, you may feel that after much consideration, you were willing to discount your price for this buyer or prospective client, which can be a good business decision.

This discount was a great business decision. Here is an actual situation where I made the decision after careful consideration to give a discount.

A young couple, let us call them John and Sue, approached me and told me they really liked who I was and how I handled things; however, they were concerned about finances and moving into a new property. They told me they wanted to give me the first opportunity, but only if I would do it for the same price as a discount agent they had spoken with.

Obviously, I was not happy about the prospects of discounting myself; however, I did like this young couple and thought I could work with them well and decided to look at what they were trying to sell and consider what my timeline and financial costs may have to be to have success with this transaction.

I had a look at what they were selling. I did like them. I liked what they had to sell and decided to give them the discount they were asking for, and here is what happened.

---

### Transaction

I gave them the discount they asked for and sold their home without another agent. I received the entire amount of the fee for my services.

### Transaction

I sold them into a new home and received the full fee for my services.

### Transaction

When it came time for them to make their next move, they called me. I sold their home, the one I had sold them into. I did give them another discount and received a fee for my services.

---

**Transaction**

When they again decided to make another move as their family was growing, I sold them into a brand-new home that was under construction and received a fee for my services as well. I sold them out of the house that they were in.

**Transaction**

They referred me to a relative. I sold their relative their first home and received a fee for my services.

**Transaction**

John and Sue sold their home to a relative of their neighbor. But they called me to help them find their new home, and I received a fee plus a bonus when they purchased their new property.

**Transaction**

I sold John and Sue's home, the last one I had sold them into, gave them another discount, and received a fee for my services.

**Transaction**

I sold them into their forever home, valued at over $1,000,000. I received a fee for my services, and 12 years later, they are still living there.

I completed eight transactions with them. I had the privilege of working with a fantastic couple over the years. I stayed connected with them and watched their three children grow from babies to young adults.

This all came about because I made a business decision to give them the discount they were asking for. And, of course, they continued to use me. I did an excellent job for them and continued to give them the same discount I had initially.

I received paychecks over the years from this young couple because of my business decision. It also allowed me to market myself every time I sold one of the homes. Was this a good business decision? I believe it was. Would I do it again? If the circumstances were the same, yes.

You need to look at each situation individually and decide if you think a discount is going to work to your benefit or not. If it's not going to benefit you, why would you give the discount? And I'd like to say, don't listen to the naysayers! This is your business, and you have the right to conduct it as you want. Some things are better kept to yourself.

## *What if you don't want to give a discount?*

If you decide not to give a discount, here are a few strategies you can use to keep the potential buyer's business.

---

### Number One

If you acknowledge the request. Here is where you show them your value and sell yourself, your service, and your product.

### Number Two

Just say "no." No, I am sorry, I don't give discounts. But what can you do for them? This is where you may want to offer some sort of a win for the prospective buyer. You want them to feel valued by you.

### Number Three

Ask them why. You want to understand why they're asking for a discount. When you can understand why it may help you to discover whether you are going to be giving them the discount or not. Is there some way that you can help them?

### Number Four

Compromise with the client. If you discount, what will that do for you and them?

---

## Number Five

You could ask what would need what would you need to have happened to make my price worth what I quoted you. This will allow you to once again show your worth and give added value if you choose.

## Number Six

You could respond with I hear you. The best products and services programs are often more expensive. Here you are showing them yes, it costs much more because it is worth it.

## Number Seven

Can you offer a payment plan? If that works for your business model, ask them what would work for their budget.

## Number Eight

Is the price the only reason the buyer is not moving forward? Possibly the price is an issue but not only the issue. Be sure to be listening to what your prospective buyer or client is telling you. Ask if they have ever purchased a service or product like what you are offering. It could be that they need to be fully aware of your offering, and they may have no idea of the cost or the value.

**Number Nine**

Give examples of what others had thought of your product or service and when they were happy and successful, whatever that may be for them.

---

## *Discovery journal*

- What are some ways you could deal with someone when they are asking for a discount?

Another motivational quote, this time from Stephen Covey.

"I am not a product of my circumstances; I'm a product of my decisions."

...

"I don't know the word 'quit.'
Either I never did, or I have abolished it."
Susan Butcher

## 5

---

# THE PROSPECTIVE CLIENT SAYS NO, SO NOW WHAT?

"Mondays are the start of the work week which offers new
beginnings 52 times a year!"
David Dweck

What are you going to do with the prospect that is not ready
to jump in with their heck yes and move forward with you?
Are you going to be able to stay in contact with them? If so,
how do you plan to do that?

Even if this prospect has entered into business with another
person, you will still want to stay in contact with them if it is
appropriate. The only time you do not have contact with the
prospect is if they have specifically asked you not to do so

So, let us assume all is good and you're going to keep in
contact with your prospect. Now how are you going to do

that? What steps are you going to take? What will your timelines be?

Here are a few ways you can nurture your relationship with your prospective client or buyer so that when they are ready, they will think of you. Your name or product will be top of their mind.

**Systems are the key!**

You will need to develop a system that will work for your business, so you don't just let your leads float away.

Do you use a client relationship management system quite often known as a CRM. These systems are incredibly important for your business. You may only have a few clients and think it's a waste of your time and resource to invest in one, but you would be dead wrong.

You will have all the best intentions to follow up with your prospect, but then life happens. We will deal with what is right in front of us now today. The busier you get when you finally come up for air, it could be days, weeks, or even months since anybody has heard from you.

Or worse, you have entirely forgotten about the potential client, and they, in turn, have forgotten about you. You will need to find a system that works for you and your type of business. A system that will make your life easier and thus keep your name at the top of your prospective client's mind.

I love the automation of the CRM system in the sense of daily reminders for keeping in contact with potential clients and buyers.

**What information should you be keeping?**

First, be sure your information collection does not appear to be an interrogation. Through your conversation, just make notes about things that seemed important. Then one day, when they contact you could pull up their information in your file system before responding, and you will be like a long-lost friend. Your connection will be warm, not cold, and with the warm connection, you will be able to move quickly towards helping them with their knees.

Here I would just like to say that be sure you are in compliance with the privacy legislation for your area so that you do not end up in hot water down the road.

**Make note of...**

- Their name.
- Where they live.
- Contact information.
- Spouse/partner's name.
- Kid's names, if appropriate.
- Pets name, if appropriate.
- What they do for a living.
- If you know their hobbies
- Anything they really like or really dislike.
- Birthdates.

- Anything you deem to be important for future information down the road.

As much information as you can about your prospect. How will you gather it? In conversations mostly that you have with them. Make notes when you hang up the call or go to your car after the meeting is over. That way, when you do connect with them, it will be helpful, and as I said, you will become that long-lost friend once again.

## *Discovery journal*

- Now is the time to write down as many things as you can think of that would be important for you to know about your prospective client in regard to your type of business or the product that you sell.

## *How many ways to keep in contact?*

What can you send them by email? First, remember depending on your area, be sure to know the rules with regard to contacting them. The last thing you want is a complaint with your privacy commissioner. Always be sure to ask their permission to contact them before sending out emails. This is best to get this consent in writing and make sure you keep it in a safe file.

Once you have received their permission, then you can decide what type of information to use to keep them informed and keep your name or product in front of them.

You can use blogs, daily affirmations, positive quotes, newsletters or just general content. Be careful not to bombard them with too many emails that will cause them not to read them and eventually unsubscribe you.

Whatever you send, make sure it is of value to that person. Always ask yourself if this will bring value. If there is no value, then do not send it. Get creative and think out of the box.

You can use your regular postal system. Now many of you may be thinking, well, that is a lot of work as well. There is a cost attached to mailing your prospects something to their address. However, I can tell you that this is one of the most powerful ways to keep in contact with your prospect. They will feel special receiving something in the mail from you.

And guess what? No one else or very few will do it. So that will set you apart from everyone else. You want to be different from everyone else. Trust me, you send them something in the mail to their home or place of address, and they will remember you forever.

***What could you send them in the mail?***

Thank you, cards. Thank you for meeting with me. Thank you for being so nice to me at that workshop. Whatever the situation was, a quick thank you note is personal, and they will appreciate receiving it. Don't we all like to be shown gratitude and be thanked?

Be sure to drop in business cards; two are usually best with whatever you send. You want them to know who sent it and how to reach you. This is not the time to be asking directly for business. You are simply saying thank you.

Sending two business cards is a very soft way of saying, "oh, don't forget me, and this is what I do." Also, they can keep one and give another to a friend.

Super great tip! Ready!

**Please use your handwriting and do not type it out!**

Thank you, cards should always be handwritten. This type of communication is meant to be personal and shows that you care enough by taking the time hand write the message on the card, the envelope addresses, and even your return address. Nothing should be typed.

And lastly, make sure it has a live stamp on it. Don't use your bulk mail to send it. They will notice this, and it will defeat the purpose.

Send a sample of your business. You can send them offers in the mail. Promotions of what you may have come up with. Or a brochure for something you are selling. Depending, of course, on what you are selling, you could also send them a sample in the mail.

Yes, it will cost you something, so be careful to keep your costs in check. If it is small and cost-effective, it can have an extremely large impact on your prospect.

Birthday cards, anniversary cards, you get the idea. And if you have collected and saved their information from your CRM system, you can set up an auto-notification for weeks or months in advance so that they will be impressed and touched that you remembered them.

Be sure to remember that if you are sending a personal card such as a birthday or anniversary card, do not include sales promotional material. That will take away from them feeling special. And you will just be one of "those salespeople" instead of someone who cares.

### *Discovery Journal*

- While it is fresh in your mind, write out what types of things you can send in the mail.
- Little things can make all the difference.
- What do you have that you could pop in the mail to your prospect?

### *How to use social media?*

Join groups. Participate. Be seen… you want and need to be seen. Just joining is not enough. You need to engage in whatever is happening within the group. Making sure you are being heard as well as being seen is one thing, but actually seeing you in a video and hearing you speaking is another. Being seen and being heard are both imperative to your business's success.

Be real. If you like something that you see, then like it. If you dislike something, zip it and be quiet, as quiet as a little mouse. Do not ever get caught up in anything that's going to cause you to look bad. Even if you disagree and there is no problem disagreeing with someone or something. However, pick your battles wisely.

I would strongly suggest that you stay out of the war and sit on the sidelines. You never know who your prospective buyer or client is and the last thing you want to do is have them see you in a conflict on social media and decide they do not want anything to do with you or your product.

Protect your reputation. Do not allow tagging without your permission. Be careful what you allow to be posted. Keep things positive and avoid any controversy or controversial topics.

Social media can help you. It can make you, or it can break you. You do not want to have worked so hard to build a following and a good reputation only to have it gone in a flash. Social media can be a very good friend or a nasty enemy.

It's not enough to just like things and give little comments as well. Remember to keep it short and positive. If you think that babies, doggies, kitties, or whatever is cute, then say so. You want people to see your name and your comments. Be sure, though, that you always keep it positive.

Praise people. Support them. Give thanks. Give gratitude to. People. Show them you care. Give your support as much as you can. Send them private messages if that is more appropriate. And be real. People will remember you and appreciate your kindness. Be creative, give value, be helpful, make it all about them, and show that you are someone who cares.

People will remember how you make them feel. If you make them feel good, they will remember you with fondness.

### *Discovery Journal*

- Write down all the social media that you would like to join and come up with a plan to set up your profiles and get started.

Warren Buffett is a very smart man. Here is a favorite quote from him.

"It is not necessary to do extraordinary things to get extraordinary results."

...

"If you really look closely, most overnight successes
took a long time."
Steve Jobs

# 6

## WHAT DO YOU REALLY WANT?

"If you really want to do something, you'll find a way. If you don't, you'll find an excuse."
Jim Rohn

Where do you want to go? Such an important question that we should be asking ourselves on a regular basis. Where do I want to go? What do I really want in life? How do I want my business and my personal life to flow now and into the future?

I'm sure you've heard or have read about goal setting and how important it is for your future. You may have been told you should have one-year goals, five-year goals, and even ten-year goals. I completely agree with that time frame for goals. It is super important to decide what you want in life and where you see yourself in the future. Most importantly, how would you like to see your life unfold?

I have set goals that were achievable, as well as some that seemed more like a dream. I wrote all of my goals down in my journal and reviewed them on a regular basis. And it's amazing how often many of those goals and dreams I have already accomplished in my life. Even ones that seemed unattainable where if I had shared them with others, they would have told me not to be silly. You cannot do that.

I love this quote by Tony Robbins, which really resonates with me and moves me to take a positive step forward.

"Setting goals is the first step in turning the invisible into the visible."

I knew I needed to set goals for myself if I was going to be able to achieve the life I wanted to create. This was an important step I knew was going to move me toward my success. What about today? It is fun to set those wild and crazy goals to dream big, and you should dream big. You should have those goals that make you reach for the stars.

However, for now, let us focus on goals and dreams you really want to achieve over a shorter period of time.

Here I want you to think on a smaller scale. Laser in on what you want to happen tomorrow in the next 30 days from now and up to the next 90 days.

Should you have goals that you want to reach years from now? For sure, you should. But right now, let us bite off a little bit at a time. If you are struggling to make sales in the end, if your income is tight, and if you are in a state of panic and frustration, then this is the time to get clear on your short-term goals and how you can achieve them.

It can be hard to look at the big picture when you are living in fear of what is going to happen not a year from now but tomorrow. If you are feeling like this, you are most likely living in survival mode, and let's get you out of that mode out of that negativity and move forward into the positive and get some money in your bank account.

I know your struggle; I was there. I remember being so broke I could not even replace the headlight in my car, let alone put food on the table. For the first team first 18 months of my business, I ended up going to food banks, went bankrupt, and had to go on government welfare just to feed my kids. It was a discouraging, depressing, terrible time in my life.

But it was this troubled time that got me going in the right direction because I decided not to give up. I knew I could do it; I just had to figure out how.

### *What can short-term goals do for you?*

Short-term goals can...

- Bring you immediate relief from your now situation.
- Bring you motivation.
- Help you organize your time so that you are more productive.

- Assist you in keeping on top of your resource because you'll have a plan.
- Guide you in the direction you need to go.
- It will give you a sense of control over your business and your personal life.
- You will begin to have clarity and come out of the confusion.
- You will be building confidence.
- You will be inspired.

What do you need to happen sooner rather than later?

This may not seem super sexy, but hey, this is where you are, so let us get some relief from your daily stress first before you start dreaming about the Mercedes-Benz.

Increments of 30 days can keep you on track and your goals attainable. Only you can take the action steps that are needed. I cannot make you do it, and your boss can't make you do it, your clients can't make you do it, and your spouse or partner can't even make you do it. You are the one who is responsible, so now is the time to step up and take action.

Will you...

- Write a business plan.
- Have your branding for your company or your product completed.
- Start your CRM.
- Hire A coach or find a mentor.
- Attend a class or a workshop or a seminar.

- Have professional photos taken if you need photos.

### *Discovery Journal*

- Now is a great time to get your journal out and write down where you see yourself in the next 30 days.
- What do you want to achieve in this short time frame?

Be realistic while you are setting these goals. You do not want to set your short-term goals so high that you cannot reach them. You do not want it to seem like a struggle. Your short-term goals should fuel your ambition. Get fired up and excited about the direction that you are heading in.

Short-term goals are needed to get to those big goals. If you can obtain your smaller short-term goals, that will set you up to obtain your massive, more exciting goals. The amazing value that your short-term goals will bring you is keeping you on track for achieving your long-term dreams for your life.

### *So, what will you accomplish in the next 30 days?*

Will you...

- Have any new clients or any clients at all.
- Have your marketing pieces ready to go.
- Have your program written.
- Have any sales in your funnel.

- Have your presentation polished and prepared.
- Will you be making any money.
- Building momentum.

Nothing builds more momentum than seeing yourself achieving what you set your mind to. Even when they are small, a win is a win. And you need those wins to keep your momentum and motivation flowing.

Once you have achieved one goal, then you achieve another goal and then another goal. You will feel unstoppable your imagination will soar with new big and larger goals because you will believe that you can do it. You can achieve what you desire.

Your goals will be bigger and bolder because you will know that you really are worthy of all your heart desires. You always knew it. Maybe you just couldn't accept it for yourself except that you can have it all. You deserve it, and you are worth it.

### *What will you do in the next 30 days?*

Will you...

- Have your social media up and running.
- Have your website ready to go.
- Are you prepared to launch your business or your product?
- Are you ready to send information to your prospective clients and buyers?

- Are you going to be having any clients working with you?
- Are you ready to receive income from all your efforts?
- Will you bring on any administration help or any assistance?

### *Why is it important to write down your goals?*

Forbes magazine quoted a Harvard MBA program in which Harvard studied goal setting with their Harvard graduate students. This is what they found...

3% of the students had written goals.

13% of the students had goals, but they were not written down, and their goals were in their minds.

84% of the students had no goals at all.

Ten years later, Harvard interviewed these students to see how they had progressed.

The 13 students who had goals in their minds but not written down earned twice the average amount of the 84% who had no goals.

The 3% who did have written goals earned an average of 10 times as much as the entire 97% combined.

The evidence is clear if you write down your goals, you will have a greater chance to achieve them and ultimately be successful in all that you dream of doing.

### *Discovery Journal*

- What are your dreams? The dreams that make you that you may be too afraid to share with anyone.
- Write the story of what you want your life to be like when you are living the life that you've always dreamed of living.

"You are never too old to set another goal
or dream a new dream." CS Lewis

...

"Almost everything worthwhile carries with it some sort of risk, whether it's starting a new business, whether it's leaving home, whether it's getting married, or whether it's flying into space."
Chris Hadfield

# 7

---

# TIME TO TAKE ACTION!

"Do not wait for the perfect time and place to enter,
for you are already onstage."
Unknown

Are you feeling stuck, feeling overwhelmed, and not sure
how to move forward?

When you are overwhelmed, you may not be thinking
clearly. Even the smallest of obstacles can look like
mountains. You may feel like you are in a dark hole without
a lighter ladder to climb out.

I remember feeling that way myself, especially at the
beginning of my sales career. Sitting at my desk, staring
down at a pen and paper, and feeling super overwhelmed and
completely lost, I had no idea what I should be doing.

Yes, I had a sales manager who gave me some guidance and tips on getting out there and making a sale, but that was it. There was no hand-holding showing me how I was entirely on my own. No one was leading the path, and it was a terrifying time, and I felt very much alone.

The industry I was in was unbelievably competitive. Although my coworkers were friendly people and thoughtful, they certainly were not going to share all their tools and years of expertise with me. I really was on my own.

Have you ever experienced a time when you could feel that you were going in alone, and it was up to you and you alone to figure it out?

Developing a success routine will get you closer to where you want to be faster than strong willpower. Positive thinking or just trying to motivate yourself does help, but it is only part of the solution. Getting into a success routine and sticking to it will help you accomplish your goals and achieving your goals will give you the best motivation you will need to keep going.

**Discovery Journal**

- Now would be a good time to write out what motivates you to take action.
- Write down the things you enjoy that you feel moving toward your success.

### *You are your own boss!*

As an entrepreneur, you do not have a boss standing over you with a big stick, making you do certain things at a certain time. You have no one watching when you come and when you go. Chances are you work from home, and no one is watching to hold you accountable. You are your boss.

Many entrepreneurs work from home, as I now do. This means you are not in an environment that may inspire you or motivate you when you are feeling down or overwhelmed. As an entrepreneur working from home, you may be spending a lot of time alone. And it's really important to find out what motivates you and what will move you to take action and continue taking the action you need to succeed for your business.

Working from home can be an amazing experience and a great benefit if you can work on your own and be motivated. However, if you're someone who needs to get those dishes done, needs to take that pet for a walk, needs to return phone calls, need to start dinner early, need to get the laundry done, wants to wash the floor, or just really wants to be able to watch your daytime soap opera then trust me you are going to fail!

Years ago, I attended a seminar, and something the speaker said really stuck with me. The speaker said we work eight hours a day for survival, and every hour after that is towards our success.

So really be real with yourself. How much time do you actually work? Not scrolling the Internet, watching YouTube videos, but actually working. If you are not putting in the time, you will not become successful. It is just the way it is.

What will taking action do for you? Well, taking action will move you toward your desires.

Every action, even an action that you feel is not significant, will start the energy to flow. No matter if it's a big or a small action, it is going to move you toward your goal. You need to start the energy flow and keep it flowing.

Jack Canfield, the author of Chicken Soup for the Soul, says, "the universe rewards those who take action. When you take action, not only do additional resources come your way, but you get feedback that helps you adjust your course and refine your approach. Taking action is one thing that separates successful people from everyday people in life."

Creating successful habits begins with taking action. Success is a lifelong journey, and your new successful behavioral habits will be the tools that will keep you right on track.

### Is it time for you to get into a successful routine?

Do you have a daily success routine? If you do, what does that routine look like? And if you do not have one is time to start one get on track with the success routine that will work for you and your business.

Take action with the basics.

- Do you have business cards? If not, get them designed and off for printing.
- Design your social media Marketing and get started with promoting yourself and your offer.
- What is happening with your website? Do you have one? If not, maybe this is the time to get started.
- Get your mailing list started. Who is going to be on that list? What will you begin to send them?
- Research others who are successful at what you are going to be doing or what you are selling. What can you learn from them?
- Are you ready to connect with your potential client? What will you begin to say to them? What is the marketing material you were ready to give them?
- Do you have a filing system prepared to keep you organized?
- Do you have a database? Start it to keep track of your clients or potential clients.
- Do you know your product inside and out? How can you transfer your enthusiasm to the potential client?

## *Discovery Journal*

- Write out ten action steps that can get you moving today toward your goals.

"Take action! An inch of movement will bring you closer to your goals than a mile of intentioned."
Steve Maraboli

## *Start with the little things.*

You are sitting at your desk. Now what? What are the little things you can do to get your momentum started? What can you do to get started that is easy and inexpensive? If you are feeling overwhelmed and the cost of things is just too much, then do the little things. Anything of which you can think. Action creates flow and energy, which develops into momentum.

## *Discovery Journal*

- Read the questions below and reflect on each question and make notes that you can refer back to, which may help to give you some clarity in your business and personal life.
- What is your why?
- Why are you doing what you're doing?
- What is the drive that got you here?
- Who is your ideal client?
- Well, what do you have to offer to be helpful to them?
- What is your business story?
- What do you have that connects with others?
- How will you serve others?
- What lights up your soul?
- What are your unique gifts?
- What causes you not to sleep at night?

Are you feeling stagnant? Like water, you will become stagnant without movement. Taking action is your next step in moving toward the success and dreams that you have been longing for. When you take action, you will find that doors will begin to open, and opportunities will present themselves to you.

The universe will reward you for taking action.

### *The law of attraction*

Have you ever felt things just flowing in your life? A time when things just seem to be working out for you? That is when you have the law of attraction working for you.

Some people think all you need to do is think positively, and things will magically start to happen for you. Well, your mindset is certainly important, but it is only part of the process. Once you have your mindset in check, then you will need to start to take action.

I am sure you've heard the phrase God helps those who help themselves. This is the same with the law of attraction and action. When you start to take action, just doing something, anything, you can move towards what it is that you want. The law of attraction recognizes your action and brings you things that will help you along the way.

...

"Even if you are on the right track, you'll get run over if you just sit there."

Will Rodgers

# 8

## BE AN OBSERVER

"Our greatest weakness lies in giving up.
The most certain way to succeed is always to try
just one more time."
Thomas Edison

What do successful salespeople do to ensure their business continues to flourish and grow over the years? If you are in sales, you should study those who have come before and after you and succeed in reaching the success you crave.

***Watch what they do.***

- How do they dress.
- How many hours a day are they working.
- What are they using for marketing?
- Where are they marketing themselves?
- How do they speak slowly, loudly, or softly.

- Read their public testimonies and what are others saying about them.
- What charities do they support?
- Search them on social media, and what do you find?
- Check out their websites.
- Google them, where they rank, and what comes up.

The point here is not to emulate them but to discover what they do and if you find something that resonates with you, then adopt that for your business as well.

*Here are the TOP SALES TIPS that I used to grow my business.*

---

**BE PREPARED**

No matter whether you are just starting out or you have been in sales for a long time, you need to be prepared prior to answering your phone and talking to a prospective client or buyer. If you are not prepared, you'll lose the opportunity to make a great first impression.

They are contacting you because they need something from you. Either your services or a product you sell, they are not calling to chat about life!

How can you be prepared? Ask yourself what kinds of questions the prospective client or buyer may want to ask. Practice with a friend or family member, or another salesperson. Once you understand what questions you may be answering, you will be able to answer them with certainty and confidence. This is how you give an excellent first impression and earn a client or buyer for life.

## TIME MANAGEMENT

Spend a week writing down everything you do, from the time you wake up until the time you go back to bed. Once you have done this, you will be able to look back over your week and see exactly what you have been doing with your time. Wasting it or using it wisely.

We all have the same 24 hours in a day. Our success will depend on how we use that time. You will be able to see easily what time-wasting tasks you are doing or time-wasting socializing. You can then make positive adjustments to your time and schedule.

When I was building my sales career, I was consistently the first one in the office in the morning and quite often the last one to leave. I found I got more done when the office was quieter. I do not have to fight for the office equipment, my time was used wisely, and there was a calm flow to what I was doing.

If you work from home, you may have to work hard to ensure you are using your time wisely. Close your office door. Do not allow family members to come in and disturb you if not important. If you find you are distracted and do not have a company office to go to, then head to your library or maybe rent an office space. Whatever you do, you must be sure your working time is being used working!

## AFTER THE SALE, FOLLOW-UP CARE

This one is done. Moving on to the next! This is the typical attitude of many salespeople. Paycheck received, deal done, sale completed, file this one away. But is your buyer or client ready to file you away?

Depending on the type of transaction you are involved in with your client or buyer, it may have been intense in terms of the amount of time you were communicating and working together. Daily phone calls, text messages, emails, or even face-to-face meetings may have been happening. This could have been over days, weeks, or even months!

Don't just 'divorce' them! Gradually lessen the communication over time. If you immediately drop them, and they don't hear from you again, then one day, they need your assistance again, and you most likely will not get the call. Why? Because you dropped them, and they noticed! And it did not feel good. Remember, people work with who makes them feel good.

I am not suggesting that you need to become a best friend, not at all. But gradually reduce the contact. Instead of communicating daily, they go weekly for four weeks and then monthly for a while, and then every few months.

Reach out even with a text and say, "Hi, just checking in that all is well." Drop a card in the mail. Drop a gift at their home or office.

If you do this, you will have a fan for life, and fans will recommend your service or product to their loved ones, friends, and associates. And the goal is to build a long-term sustainable business by referral.

**BE THE EXPERT**

Set yourself up to be the expert. Prospective clients and buyers want to work with the expert because they need to have the services of a person who knows everything about what they want to buy or are wanting to do. They are not the experts, and that is why they have come to you. Because you are.

How do you set yourself up to be one? It is easy. Research and learn everything there is to know in terms of what you are selling or offering them.

For example, if you are a life coach, what will you be teaching? What else are others in the industry discussing? What is treading? How will it help them? If they do not take your program, how will that cost them their lives?

If you are a real estate agent, how can you be the expert? Research your area, know what is selling, what is not selling, and what locations to stay away from. Where are the schools and community centers? How far are shopping, hospitals, and emergency services? What is new being built in the area? Visit every open house you can. You need to know as much as you possibly can so that you can easily answer questions asked of you.

What product are you selling? Same as the other two examples, learn everything you can about what you are selling. Research your competition; what are they offering?

Becoming an expert is knowledge, and only you can gather this knowledge for yourself.

## DEVELOP A SYSTEM

Systems are key! When you find a system that works for you, repeat it daily. There are sales systems you can purchase that might help you, but I believe designing your own system is best.

You know you and your prospective client or buyer best. Develop a system on how you can attract them to you, your marketing, your website, or your product.

Once you get a system that works for you, be careful to drastically change it. If it works, do not reinvent the wheel, you may find you lose your momentum and, in turn, lose those clients or buyers.

## BE ON TIME

Nothing is worse than being late! Late for an appointment, a video call, or a phone call. Be there, ready to go, when you agreed to. When you are late, it screams, you are not important to me.

If you are someone who, for whatever reason, is late on a regular basis, fix it! Stop it! It's a habit, and there is no reason for it. I am not talking about being stuck in traffic due to an accident on the road. I am talking about being sloppy with your time and not caring about being on time.

If you have an appointment with someone away from your home or office, arrive early. Typically, I am anywhere from 30 to 15 minutes early for my appointments. If I am driving, I take this time to relax in my car and surf the net, listen to podcasts or chat on the phone.

If it is a video call or scheduled phone call, again, I am ready at the very least 15 minutes before the scheduled time.

Make being on time a new positive habit!

## MESSAGING AND SELF-PROMOTION SHOULD BE PERSONAL

What is the message you are putting out into the world about you, your business, and or your product?

Clear messaging is vital for your business! If your message in any way is confusing, the prospective client or buyer may pass right by you due to their confusion about you and what you do or sell. And if they are confused, it is your fault. It is your message that is confusing them.

I collaborate with people to clarify their business stories and personal messaging to ensure there is no confusion in what you are saying about your product, your business, or your services.

Your message, whether it is in a story format, social media, or a type of print advertising, must be structured so that the prospective buyer or client is drawn to you and your story.

Your message is going to tell them why they need to buy or product or work with you. Not directly but indirectly and subtly. You want them to feel you. And when they feel your message or story, they want to reach out to learn more about you, your service, or your product.

Not everyone is going to want to work with you, and really, in the end, you'll find that is a blessing. Direct your messaging and story towards those you want to attract and draw to you.

**BE A PROBLEM SOLVER**

Early on in my career, I knew I needed to figure out how to be a better problem solver. In order to get the sale firmed up, there were problems, usually small but some big, that had to be dealt with. Even the smallest problem could kill the sale once emotions got the best of the buyer or prospective client.

Be calm when problems arise. Once, I was selling a brand-new housing development on a golf course, so you can imagine the homes were fairly pricy. Buyers would pick their lot, decide on which home they wanted, order upgrades and do a fair amount of customizing.

I arrive at work on a Saturday morning only to have a stressed-out husband and wife, buyers, waiting for me. They told me that the wrong house was being built on their lot, not the house they ordered.

I met them at the house, and sure enough, it was the wrong house. Inside I was freaking out, not knowing how this mistake had happened and worried I did it! If they did not want this house, this was going to be a costly mistake.

I looked at them and said, "Well, do you like this house?" After a few minutes, they said, well, we like the windows in this design. Long story short, they decided they liked this house better than the one they chose, with a few changes agreed to by the developer. Problem solved.

Just for your interest, the error happened by the developer typing in the wrong code for the house design!

---

Almost all problems can be solved. Stay calm, think outside the box, and, if you need to, reach out to experts that can help your clients or buyers make an informed decision.

...

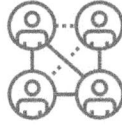

"The real test is not whether you avoid this failure because you won't. It's whether you let it harden or shame you into inaction, or whether you learn from it; whether you choose to persevere."
Barack Obama

# 9

## WHAT IS YOUR STORY?

"I never look back, darling. It distracts from the now."
Edna Mode

Have you ever sat down and thought about what my story is? Has anyone ever asked you hey, "what's your story?" We all have a story. Our life is a book, and inside that book or the chapters of our lives. And it is these chapters that allow us to move forward our holds us back from achieving what we dream of achieving.

If these chapters are holding us back, and most chapters of our life can do that, we have to learn how to rid ourselves of these limiting beliefs and past situations, whatever the trauma may have been. It is time to release ourselves from what does not serve us in the life we have today.

There are many studies out today that you can find if you Google the Internet about how often we are thinking negative thoughts.

One study I remember reading about says that we think approximately 70,000 to 80,000 thoughts daily. Of those 70,000 to 80,000 thoughts, 60% of those thoughts will be negative thoughts. The amazing thing I found about this is that 60% of negative thoughts we are thinking are actually repetitive thoughts that we think on a daily basis!

Wow! That is a lot of negativity to overcome in our daily lives with just our thinking patterns.

This thinking pattern starts from the time that we are children. Depending on the negative messages that we were being told, seeing, or feeling growing up as a child. Those messages can still cause problems in our lives today.

The positive thing is that we can overcome these negative thoughts, the ones that are repetitive day after day, month after month, and year after year. These negative thoughts will hold you back from living the life you have always dreamed of living. It will hurt your business, cause conflict in your relationships, and you may feel unworthy of having anything good in your life, which can include money.

***What do you find you are saying on a regular basis?***

Pay attention to what you are saying to yourself, then pay attention to what you are saying to others. When you make a mistake, do you call yourself stupid or dumb? Many of us do that, but that is not a very nice way to speak to ourselves, and we probably wouldn't speak to others that way as well, so it's time to start respecting ourselves and speaking kindly to ourselves.

### *What are you saying to other people?*

I had a friend years ago that went through a nasty divorce, and all I heard was about the divorce and about how badly they were treated and how sad it was and how frustrating it was, and how angry the entire situation was. My friend could go on for a good hour repeating this story almost on a regular basis every time we would meet.

We did not see each other for a number of years. We lost touch, and about ten years later, we connected and decided to have coffee.

Well, within five minutes of chatting, my friend starts on the exact same story told years and years ago. It was almost word for word! I can tell you that this friend of mine was still in the exact same place they were financially, relationship-wise, mentally, and physically as they were ten years previously.

I finally cut ties with this friend because I could not take the negativity anymore. And I always felt bad because I knew that reliving this past was not benefiting my friend in any way. It was only hindering.

So, what about you? What stories are you telling yourself or telling others? And if you are not sure, all you have to do is ask a good friend that you can trust or a family member. Ask them whether you tend to repeat anything. Is there a story and a negative story that I repeat time and time again? And if there is, then you need to change that ASAP.

### Are you living the same 30 days over and over again?

When I was growing up, my family life was very chaotic. Both my father and my mother were Alcoholics. There was always a lack of money, lots of fighting, and lots of negative messages. It was not a healthy environment for children to grow up in, that was for sure.

Later in life, my mom had some dark demons, but she never did deal with them. She kept them hidden in the closet and refused to do anything about them, and they were so dark that they were tearing her down inside to the point where she was not functioning well in life.

We grew up on the government welfare system, and my mom was on the welfare system until the day she died. It would start where we would get the check, life would be good, groceries would be bought, and we would have a little bit of fun. The kids would get a treat, and everything would be great for about two weeks.

Then the money would be gone, and the yelling would happen, and this stress would happen, and the screaming would happen. My mom would be borrowing money and going to food banks, trying to figure out where to get cash so that she could feed us kids. Then the next welfare check would come in, and it would start all over again.

I can honestly say that my mom lived the same 30 days over and over and over again. Her life very rarely was anything different. Seeing this and growing up in it certainly was my motivation for not going there and wanting to achieve the normalcy of life as well as having all the things that I always dreamed of having.

So, take a look at your life. Are you living the same 30 days over and over again? Are you living the same year over and over again? If you are, it is time to do something about it. It is a pattern that you're in, and it doesn't have to be that way.

To have success in your business, you have to change your way of thinking. You have to change your negative patterns. If you do not, it will be difficult for you, and you may end up failing.

***We have two minds.***

Did you know that you have two minds? Well, we do have our conscious mind, which is our thought process, and then we have our unconscious mind. The way I understand it is that our unconscious mind is like a filing cabinet, and that is where all our memories, good or bad or held. Our unconscious mind is also where we keep all our programs, and is why we do what we do on a daily basis. Sometimes we do not even know why we're doing things, and that's usually because we're working out the programs that are in our unconscious mind.

The positive thing is understanding this means we can change it. We can change the programs. We can clean out the files in our unconscious mind and put in new files. It does not just happen overnight, but if you start working on it little by little every single day, it will happen.

Things that were said to us when we were children if we were bullied. If a teacher picked on us, if we had an abusive parent or if something terrible or traumatic happened to us, it's going to be filed in our unconscious mind, and that's going to cause certain programs or habits of behavior and how we view ourselves. If we have our unconscious mind full of negatives and negative patterns and behaviors, we need to work on clearing them out and filling them up with positives.

Negative self-talk is one of the biggest things that is sitting in our unconscious mind. If we were told we were not good enough, all you are is trouble; then we may grow up believing those negative statements. If that is the case, it will be hard to excel in sales. Sales is a tough business and can be hard on self-esteem. It is imperative that we have a healthy mindset.

Some of the common things I heard growing up were...

- You kids caused me to drink.
- I'm broke all the time because of you damn kids.

These kinds of messages are sitting in our unconscious mind. That is where we store them, and we need to consciously work to remove them so that we can be healthy in our minds. If our mindset is healthy, life will be a lot smoother for us.

So, what kind of tools can we use to help us change what we have been filing in our subconscious mind?

Well, there are many out there. I'm going to tell you a few of the ones that I personally use that I found to be very helpful, and hopefully, you will find them helpful as well. But if these do not resonate with you, please look elsewhere for what will help you. There is a lot of help on the Internet these days. There is no excuse for us not to be able to become the healthy people that we are meant to be.

### *Turn your negative talk into positive talk.*

Your self-esteem can be impacted hugely by your self-talk, and affirmations are one of the tools that you can use to help you overcome negative talk and turn it into positive talk.

For example, if you say something like I don't deserve anything good, turn it around and start saying I deserve everything that's good. You want to flip your negative into a positive, so what is the opposite of your negative statement?

### *Start using empowering thoughts.*

I hear people so often say oh, I can't do that. I remember I even had a friend whose husband said oh, she'll never do that. If other people don't believe in you, it doesn't mean you can't do it.

It's time to use empowering thoughts and statements. If you don't know where to start, here are a few examples for you.

- I achieve my goals.
- I am responsible for the good and the bad in my life.
- I learn from my mistakes.
- I love myself.
- I am happiness.
- I am worthy of having everything I dream of having.
- I forgive my past.
- My life is just the way I want it.
- My career is successful.
- I have more than enough money.

Be sure to choose your words carefully. For example, if you wanted to lose weight, your affirmation would be I am slender, or I am the weight of ??? Even saying I am losing weight is a negative because it is affirming that you haven't lost the weight.

It is the same way with money affirmations. You want to say I have all the money that I need, and money flows to me easily and freely. I am a money magnet. Those statements are in the now, and that is what's important. Your affirmations need to be written in the now, so be careful with your words.

Write your affirmations on sticky notes and put them everywhere!

- Put them on your fridge.
- Put them on your mirror.
- Put them in your car.
- Put them in your day timer.
- Put them on your computer.

You need to be able to read them throughout the day. If you are repeating up to 60,000 negative thoughts a day, you are going to need a lot of positives to reprogram that subconscious mind of yours. Have them by your bedside table instead of looking at your phone first thing in the morning. Grab your list of positive affirmations and start reading those before reading anything else.

### *Take time to be grateful.*

Gratitude is one of the quickest ways to achieve success because when you are grateful, the universe is going to give you more things to be grateful for. Start a gratitude journal and write down as many things as you can think of to be grateful for.

Sometimes it can seem hard, especially when we are feeling like we're down and not grateful for anything, but really there are always things to be grateful for. We have food. We have air. We live in a nice country. We have friends, we have family, and we have clothing. Start to take a look at what is going on in other parts of our world, and that will quickly help you to realize how grateful you should be for who you are and what you have, and where you live.

You may find that your negative programs are so deeply buried in your mind that you need extra help to work through them. And that is great. If that is what you need, get the support, don't just ignore it.

Remember, you do not want to live the same 30 days over and over again for the rest of your life. Your life is meant to be fun and meaningful. Enjoy your time here. So, get the help that you need. Reach out. There is lots of help available to you.

Watch optimistic speeches on YouTube. There are thousands of them.

Do some meditations. You will find them on YouTube as well. You can do meditations for 5 minutes up to 60 minutes. It is really up to you.

As you go about your day, soft motivational music plays in the background. All these little things can help you to move from negative to positive.

***And stay away from negative people as much as you can.***

We are going to have negative clients from time-to-time negative coworkers, negative partners, negative children, and negative parents, and that's okay if it's from time to time. But if it is happening on a regular daily basis, you need to do something to protect yourself and move your mind away from the negative and into the positive. If that means you have to limit time with certain family members or friends, then do that. You need to protect yourself and your mindset.

Remember what you focus on in this life; you are going to attract to you. At least, that is what I believe. I believe it, and I have seen it in my own life and in other people's lives I know. Be sure you are attracting good positive things into your life and not negativity and sadness.

How do you do that? Well, you be grateful. You be positive, not only when life is good! Know that good things are coming your way, know that you are worthy of those things, and know that you deserve those things, and you will see things start to change.

Have you ever woken up on the wrong side of the bed and had a really grumpy start to the day? Guess what happens? More grumpy things come into your life for you to be grumpy about, and your day goes on and on with more irritations and more grumpiness.

Now notice that when you wake up happy and grateful with energy, typically, you are going to have a great day. Your attitude sets the mood for your day. So, give yourself an attitude check when you wake up in the morning. And if you find that you are not in a good mental state, then do what you can to change that before you get too far along in your day.

Your mindset is of the utmost importance when you are in sales. Your mindset will make or break you.

### It's time to write a new story.

When I say it's time to write a new story, that's exactly what I mean.

Get a journal. Get a pad of paper. Get a book. Get your favorite pen and sit down and start to write your life out the way you want it to unfold. Write a new story for your life. One that you can move towards.

For example, if you are having money issues and you want to write a new chapter in your life around money, you may write something like this.

I am so grateful and thankful that my yearly income is now my monthly income. Money flows to me in so many different ways. Sometimes, I go to the mailbox, and there is a check for me that I wasn't expecting. I have come to see that I'm a money magnet. I love money, and money loves me.

### New Money Story

"I am so grateful that I have the money that I need. I help my children with their education so they can get the best education they need to succeed in their lives. Help them start out by getting into their first home so that they can live a stable life for themselves and their families.

I love that I am able to help people less fortunate than me financially. I give my time, and my money to help others on this planet make their lives better and more pleasant.

I get to go on the best holidays and stay in the nicest hotels. I appreciate all the good things that money does for me and that I can do with money."

Hope this little bit helps you to see how you can rewrite your story and how rewriting your story it is going to help you with your business, selling your products, and living the life that you deserve to live. Moving you out of struggle and the poverty mindset that you may be living in.

You can do this same type of rewriting your story, and you should for your relationships, your financial goals, and how you see your personal growth folding. What does your spiritual life look like? What do you want your social life to look like? What do you want your business life to look like?

Then when you have written a new book with the chapters of your new life, you'll want to read it over on a regular basis. Carry it around with you and instead of playing games on your phone or scrolling on your phone, read your new life story.

Email it to yourself so you've got it on your phone or on your computer so that anytime you need a little bit of motivation or you want to remember what you want your life to look like, pull that story out and read it. And start reprogramming that subconscious mind of yours that is full of negative programs. Rewriting your story and reading it over daily, and feeling the excitement of it - it will start replacing the negative programs in your subconscious mind.

...

"A year from now you will wish you had started today."
Unknown

# 10

## WHAT'S NEXT?

Congratulations on moving forward with the life of your dreams!

Hopefully, you completed all of your journal entries. These entries will be excellent references to refer back to when you get stuck moving forward.

I hope you will write all the chapters of your new life in your book. You can read it over for encouragement, and so you do not forget your vision of where you want to be how you want your life to unfold.

Remember, you are always young enough to make positive changes. We are not meant to stay the same. We are meant to grow and evolve in our lives. That is what makes life so interesting and fun.

If you have not rewritten your story yet, be sure you do it, it will work magic for you in transforming your life. We all need a vision to move towards… all of us.

I believe a miracle resides in all of us, and it happens at the moment when you decide to choose success over struggle. When you decide to stop living the same 30 days over and over again, you decide to start taking responsibility for yourself for your past and future and for where you are today.

I'm excited for you. If you did everything in this book and read it entirely, then you are off to a great start! I know you're going to get there, where you want to be in your life. I know you're going to live the life you dream of, not someone else's life or someone else's dreams for you.

Be sure to celebrate yourself. Celebrate your achievements. Do something kind for you. And put yourself first for a change.

There are so many people out there searching for their purpose in life, looking outside of themselves and wondering why they're here and what their purpose is. But I believe it's very simple… you are your purpose.

You are here on this earth for you. To live your life experience. To take care of you and live the life that you we're meant to live and experience life with the rest of us.

At times people get passion and purpose confused. Your purpose is you. You are here for you, and then there is your passion. And your passion is what you search for. So, look in the mirror, and you know what you're going to see is your purpose because your purpose is you!

I hope that all of this information is going to help you along the way in promoting yourself and your business and helping you in your personal life as well.

Remember, you deserve and are worthy of living the best life this world has to offer. Don't sabotage it!

...

"Our greatest glory is not in never falling,
but in rising every time, we fall."
Confucius

# PART 2

# MEET JULIE FAIRHURST

Julie Fairhurst is a Transformational Story Coach and the Founder of the Women Like Me Program.

Julie was a certified prevention educator with the Canadian Red Cross. She has been delivering empowering workshops to adolescents and adults on the issues affecting their safety. She has presented to organizations such as the Vancouver Police Department, Justice Institute, University of British Columbia, and Capilano College. Behavioral Society of British Columbia, Surrey Memorial Hospital. Teachers Association of North Vancouver, and Shine Live, as well as appearing on television and in video.

Julie had a chaotic upbringing and thought her life was set for failure, following down the paths of her previous generations. As a young teenager, she was headed in the wrong direction, and a social worker told her, "There is no hope for you."

But, somewhere deep inside, that young girl inside her showed up and reminded her that she wanted better for her life and the life of her children. Julie had no support from anyone, not a soul. She had to do it all on her own.

Was it an easy road? No, it was far from easy. Julie was a single mom for 24 years. She and her children lived off government handouts. Julie stood in line at food banks to feed her kids. At Christmas, they received Christmas hampers, and she would go to the toy bank to get presents for her children. The path was hard to change, especially when it was all she knew. But she did it.

Julie went back to school and finished her education. She built an outstanding career in sales, marketing, and promotion. She won the company's top awards and was the first woman to achieve top salesperson year after year in a male-dominated industry. She was a sales manager for some of the country's most prestigious developers.

Some people say never to look back, but Julie does every day. Why? Because she never wants to forget the journey that led her to where she is today. And today, her life is entirely different. Julie didn't just fall into this life. She worked at it every day, all the time.

Then, in 2019, Julie's beautiful 24-year-old niece died from a drug overdose on the streets of Vancouver, Canada. And that was the day she said enough! Her niece's death indirectly resulted from the generational beliefs and abuse that some of her siblings continue with their destructive lifestyles.

Julie believes that when we don't deal with our traumas, we pass the dysfunction along to the next generation. This is what happened to her beautiful young niece. This is where her passion comes from, the reason she started Women Like Me.

Everyone can change their story, no matter what their story is right now or what it has been in the past. Everyone's story matters, and that includes yours. And we can rewrite our stories. It's not that hard to do. Reach out if I can help you.

**Want to connect with Julie?**

Email: julie@changeyourpath.ca

Women Like Me Stories

www.womenlikemestories.com

**Find Julie on Social Media:**

YouTube – Julie Fairhurst Women Like Me

https://www.youtube.com/channel/UChFnLgiUC9mWnvp7jikKBw

Women Like Me on Facebook

https://www.facebook.com/StoryCoachJulieFairhurst

Rock Star Strategies on Facebook

https://www.facebook.com/juliefairhurstcoaching

LinkedIn - Julie Fairhurst Women Like Me Stories

https://www.linkedin.com/in/womenlikemestories/

Instagram – Women Like Me Stories

https://www.instagram.com/womenlikemestories/

TikTok

https://www.tiktok.com/@womenlikemestories

...

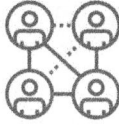

"Forget past mistakes. Forget failures. Forget everything
except what you're going to do now and do it."
William Durant

# WOMEN LIKE ME COMMUNITY

If you do not belong to Women Like Me Community – Julie Fairhurst, I would be pleased if you decided to join us.

The Women Like Me Community – Julie Fairhurst is a Facebook group of like-minded women. Women who want to pay it forward and lift others to promote healing in the world.

Ages range from 17 to 83 from all over the world and from all walks of life and all over the world.

As a community, we write community books, with the proceeds going to charity. Maybe you will join in on the next book?

Together, as a group, we can help promote healing in our world.

Join the Movement on Facebook:

Come to the community and spend time with other inspiring women. We are waiting for you!

Women Like Me Community – Julie Fairhurst

https://www.facebook.com/groups/879482909307802

...

"Character cannot be developed in ease and quiet.
Only through experience of trial and suffering can the soul
be strengthened, ambition inspired, and success achieved."

Helen Keller

# WOMEN LIKE ME BOOK SERIES

Do you have a story that needs to be told? A story that may be holding you back from living your best life. Or, possibly, you have overcome and are ready to share with the world, hoping that your story will invoke another to live a better life.

Writing is therapeutic to the soul. Writing about your past events can be beneficial, both emotionally and physically. You can increase your feelings of well-being and even enhance your immune system.

We only get one chance. Our lives are not a dress rehearsal for our next lifetime. We only get this one life, and it's here and now.

Reach me at www.womelikemestories.com and let me know you are ready to tell your story. The world is waiting for you.

**Women Like Me Stories**

https://womenlikemestories.com/tell-your-story/

"The only place where success comes before work is in the dictionary." Vidal Sassoon

# READ MORE FROM JULIE FAIRHURST

Julie's books are available on Amazon or the Women Like Me Stories website.

---

**Sales and Personal Growth**

Positivity Makes All The Difference

Agent Etiquette

7 Keys to Success – How to Become A Real Estate Badass

30 Days to Real Estate Action – Real Strategies & Real Connections

---

**Women Like Me Book Series**

Women Like Me – A Celebration of Courage and Triumphs

Women Like Me – Stories of Resilience and Courage

Women Like Me – A Tribute to the Brave and Wise

Women Like Me – Breaking Through the Silence

Women Like Me – From Loss to Living

---

**Women Like Me Community Book Series**

Women Like Me Community – Messages to My Younger Self

Women Like Me Community – Sharing Words of Gratitude

Women Like Me Community – Sharing What We Know to
Be True

Women Like Me Community – Journal for Self-Discovery

Women Like Me Community – Sharing Life's Important Lessons

www.ingramcontent.com/pod-product-compliance
Lightning Source LLC
Chambersburg PA
CBHW070934210326
41520CB00021B/6939